KERRY STRICKLAND

My Best Boss Ever

Entrepreneurship – Fact and Fiction

First edition

This book was professionally typeset on Reedsy.
Find out more at reedsy.com

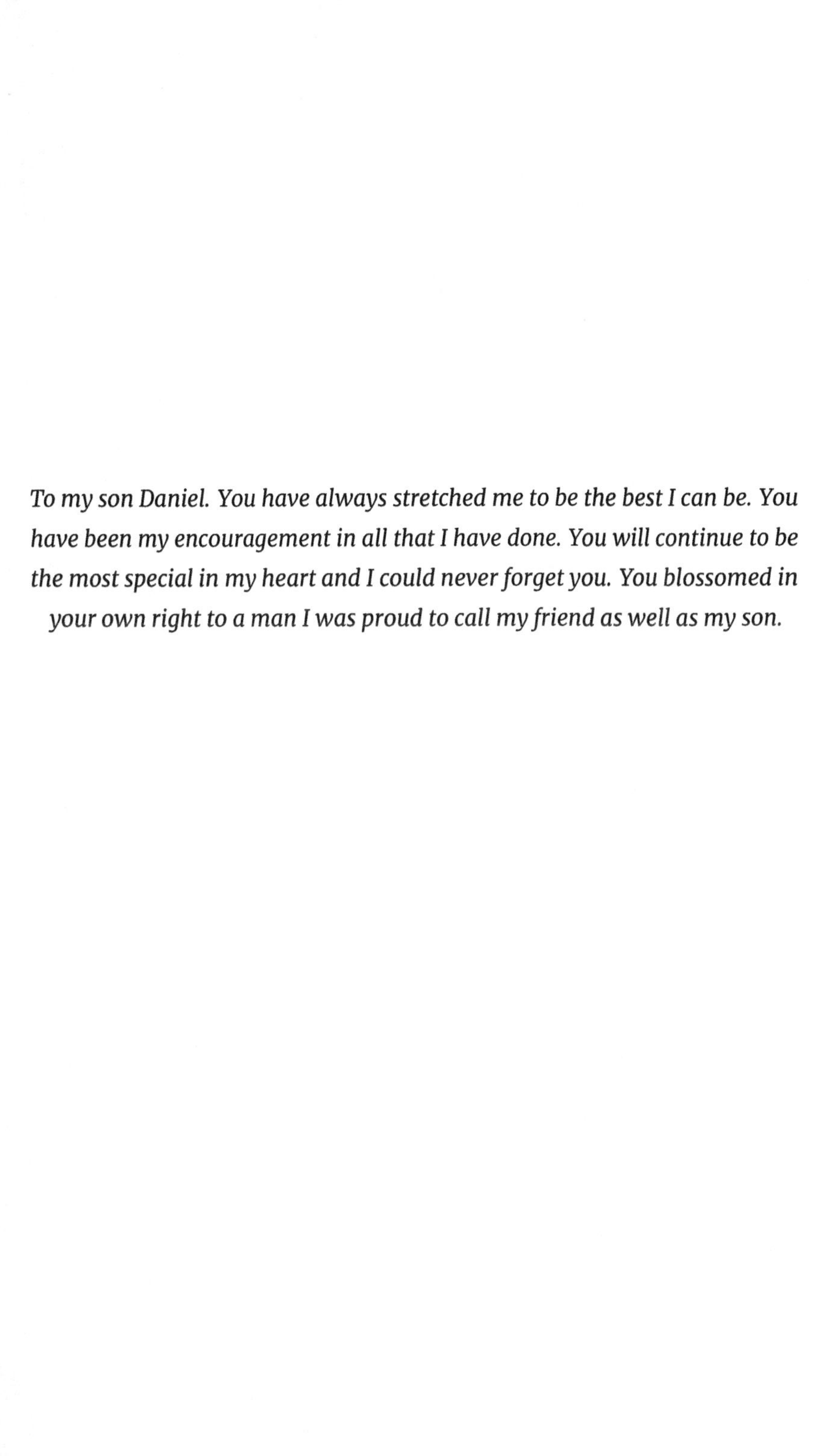

To my son Daniel. You have always stretched me to be the best I can be. You have been my encouragement in all that I have done. You will continue to be the most special in my heart and I could never forget you. You blossomed in your own right to a man I was proud to call my friend as well as my son.

Contents

Introduction	1
Everyone Wants to be Their Own Boss	6
Resources	11
Business and Financial Plan	14
Making it Legal	18
Decision Making – Easy or Hard	21
Systems	23
Hiring Anyone?	25
Bookkeeping and Accounting	29
Conclusion	31
About the Author	33

Introduction

Journey by KK Strickland

Welcome to a segment of my life and world. I am aged beyond an official "retirement age", but continue to work daily, full time; simply because I have the Best Boss Ever - ME!

I have worked for others during my life and self-employed about a third of the time. Between the two, the latter is definitely the best. Join me, as I share some of the facts and fiction about being self employed.

We will travel through the process of becoming an entrepreneur, (self-employed), beginning with your first thoughts of being your own boss. The most gigantic speed bump in this journey is getting started! How ironic.

INTRODUCTION

I must make it clear at the beginning of this text, that I subscribe to following the laws in licensing, occupancy of structures, insurance and taxes. I certainly know folks who do not follow the rules and have scoffed at me for doing so. However, I have no worries when operating illegally; never think of getting shut down or suffering tax liabilities, penalties or fees. I can attest that if I have made mistakes, they have not been intentional.

If you think that fudging on the system is smart - let me share a story. I have worked with folks who are now in their 60's and have no Social Security because they lived their lives "working under the table" which means working for cash and unreported income. The worker thinks it's great because they get the entire amount. The boss thinks it's great because they don't have to pay employee taxes or Workman's Comp, etc.

Retirement for these individuals can be a very scary journey. Typically there is little or no savings, and definitely no retirement account. Did you know that retirement accounts such as IRA or Roth IRA's are funded from reported working income? What seemed crafty and smart when young and "working under the table", now becomes stupid and frightening upon retirement.

I also want to share that when caught, the employer will be fined as well as having to pay all taxes. I used to see lists of employers who had been caught doing this and the amounts they had to pay. This must have put some of these folks out of business. The employee had to file income tax and give up the money which should have gone to their share of the employment taxes. And just maybe had to defend a charge of income-tax evasion.

Let's get started and go through a light-hearted overview of steps necessary to start and perpetuate a successful business venture - where you CAN be your own Boss!

Entrepreneurship - What is it?

Simply put, it is being self-employed. There are many facets to being self-employed. You will find yourself being the decision maker, the customer service representative, the cashier, money maker, the bookkeeper and do not forget; the janitor. Although I do have an assistant now and a payroll company and help pay my taxes, I still perform most of these duties myself. I especially enjoy hauling the garbage down one floor, out the back door of the office building, across the parking lot to the garbage bin. I repeat the process for recycling. Fun. Especially in the rain.

I find it interesting that most folks on the outside only see a little bit of the duties of the "boss". Think of an iceberg. Most of what you do will be below the surface and out of sight of almost everyone. Others will make comments to you like... "wow, you are your own boss and get to take time off whenever you want" and "I bet you are just rolling in money - you have to, cause you own your own business". I'm sure you have heard many of the fictitious comments and misconceptions people have about entrepreneurship. These are the biggest two. It is not impossible to achieve raging success, but for most at the beginning of the business venture, you are the janitor. I hope that puts it into perspective.

Some people who are self-employed can take time off when they want and they may be rolling in dough ($$) but that is not the case probably 95% of the time. Most self-employed people are folks who have dreams of doing something they are passionate about, have designed a new way of doing an established thing, thought of a brand new concept or discovered a new service to offer. What you can do is limitless and you may just be the someone who discovers something totally different or invent something new. The sky's the limit.

A lot of the time, your starting capital can limit your dreams and desires. I have not spent time in this publication to address the concept of financing your business, but rather stipulate that you have the funding you need to start a small business located in your home town or possibly on the internet. In other words, it is a small business venture at this time, but will be capable of ramping up and growing.

I can speak authoritatively to the concept of entrepreneurship with growth, as this is the course I have taken in my two successful business ventures. These two businesses, which are totally different from one another, account for 19 years of my working life. The remainder of my time was spent working mostly in the medical field. Let's move on.

Everyone Wants to be Their Own Boss

Everyone wants to be their own boss - what business do you have in mind where you can be boss?

How many times have you said, "that would make a great business idea" or "if I only had the money, I would love to turn that into a business". If you have, you are among the many who walk this earth. There is no way to know what percentage of people put their ideas into motion, but I bet it is less than 1%.

What stops us from executing our dreams and desires of running our own businesses? I bet you already know the answers to that one. How about these?

1. **I'm afraid I will fail.**
2. **I'll have to stop working and what will my family do? I will be losing important benefits.**
3. **I don't have the money to tie me over until my business makes money.**
4. **I don't know where to start.**
5. **I don't know what it will cost to start my business.**
6. **Will I need to get licenses and insurance - I have no idea how to**

do that.

7. **And so on, and so on, and so on.**

All these reasons have credibility. How could you know how to start a business if you've never done it before? That's a no brainer. The following sections will help you identify the various locations readily available to point you in the right direction. But even if you know where to start, do you think you will be able to overcome the speed bumps?

Being your own boss comes with an entirely different mindset of employment. I once had a young lady who wanted to learn the ins and outs of self-employment. She accused me of being a scammer. When I asked her why she felt that way, she said I don't expect to spend money on your coaching. You should be paying me. In my head I said "huh"? I listened to her a little while longer and thanked her for showing interest. I had to tell her, "What you have just described to me in detail is having a job, not being self-employed." This interaction really caught me off guard. I was so surprised that she would think that being self-employed would automatically come with a paycheck and benefits. Uhhhh, No.

There are certain steps you can take which do not cost anything to do.

If you are seriously interested in being your own boss, do you have a product, a service or function in mind? If you do, I suggest you write it down on a piece of paper (how antiquated) and describe your scope of involvement in detail. Don't worry about the other things an entrepreneur does - we'll talk about those later. This description will be what you think your duties will be. Keep in mind you haven't started doing research at this point.

Visualize yourself preparing for your new business. Write down what you think you will need to perform the function. It may be a room out of your home, a store-front, an office space away from the home, a street corner to park a food truck on. You get it - write down the big things you will need. Don't worry about money right now. You are just getting a feel and insight as to what your surroundings will be like.

If you are able, draw a sketch of your idea and put a picture of yourself in it performing the duties of your chosen endeavor. It can be a stick person - that's all I can draw. Maybe you could even find a picture of similar surroundings on the internet, or even go out and take a picture of it. I don't understand why, but this will bring your thoughts into the visual realm. You can now see it - it has substance and is not just a thought process which is in a continuous loop, but a reality having substance.

Now put your clients or customers in the picture too. Maybe it is one person at a time, maybe it is a room full of people. Maybe you are working with them to get a chore accomplished or teaching them what you know. Maybe you are aiding them in their daily lives or helping them get out of debt. Once again - the sky's the limit.

Entrepreneurship starts at Step #1

You can make your "idea" become real in your mind. Entrepreneurship is a viable reality and has substance and worth. Once you can visualize your dream, you are able to set your course and start digging in.

I am no psychologist, but I do know enough to share with you that visualization of who you can become and what you can accomplish, begins with visualization. Can you envision yourself as being self-employed and that entrepreneur? Success depends on execution of the picture in your mind.

Resources

Resources:

Have you ever heard the saying, "Why reinvent the wheel?" I am sure that you have. Of course this means that if you need something or need to learn something and it is already "out there" for your gathering, then be a gather-er. Don't start from scratch and waste your time. Resources are available for you to consult in almost every step of the entrepreneurial journey. I have listed a few of them here and what these resources can do for you. The majority come with no cost at all. There is a lot of free information out there. But be careful who you listen to or read. If it sounds unrealistic, find an additional source to verify what you have read or learned. There are a lot of strange ideas out there. Be sure you don't waste your time nor your money. You may even be fortunate to be able to shadow someone in the same business as you want to explore. Don't be afraid to ask.

Check out the SBA - The Small Business Administration. There are countless resources there to help you. There are even counselors and mentors who will help you every step of the way. They can help from creating a business plan, to providing loans for your start-up. Here's what their Google listing has to say.

"From the U.S. Small Business Administration –

"Our office provides help with SBA services including funding programs, counseling, federal contracting certifications, and disaster recovery. We can also help you by making referrals to our partner organizations, lenders, and other community groups that help small businesses succeed. Please contact your local SBA district office for more immediate service by clicking the "Call" button above. For general questions contact the SBA's Answer Desk at (800) 827-5722, or email answerdesk@sba.gov, on weekdays from 9 a.m. to 6 p.m. ET. F Go to SBA.gov

Yes, the SBA is a Federal Government organization. It has been around since July 30th, 1953. A lot can be learned from the SBA which has 70 years of experience. Don't reinvent the wheel!

Get on the internet and find businesses like the one you dream about, or one which is close in nature and scope. Read everything on these websites. What are the promises - how is the presentation - how much can you find out? If there is a review page, read the reviews. You can sometimes get an insight as to the problem areas or issues this business has.

Once you have done your research from home, **go out into your physical world** and find a similar business and visit them in action. If possible, quietly observe without asking any questions at first.

(I used to teach Junior Achievement Business and Personal Finance to 7th graders in my hometown. Each of the students chose a business they would like to work at one day. I asked them to visit the location (Most were headed off to McDonalds) and quietly observe everything going on. They were to take notes on the employees and their duties. They were also to observe how the employees were dressed and how they interacted with the customers. Some of the positions included the cashier, the drive-up window person, the french fry station and to see in the back where the food was being prepared. Once they observed all locations, they were to choose which of these they were most interested in applying for. *https://jausa.ja.org*)

You can do the same thing the best you can, using the tools at your disposal. In person, internet, books (library or amazon), phoning them and any other way you can think of. This is all part of your research, using all and any resources at your disposal.

Business and Financial Plan

Business Plan / Financial Plan:

The business and financial plan are two extremely important start-up segments, especially if you are planning on borrowing funds for your new business. Just these two topics alone can fill volumes by themselves. There are very formal ways of presenting this information. The www.SBA.gov website is one of the best sources in detailing how to put your information together. They offer services for laying out your business plan and preparing you and it for requesting financial assistance. The SBA also provides financial loans for business. The SBA is one of your best supports and has answers for you on how to secure financial help.

In a much less formal offering, once you have decided on your business endeavor and scope of your business, you will begin the amazing task of spelling it out. Literally. I prefer to do this with old- fashioned pencil and paper, but you can use the method of your choice to draw yourself a picture of services or products you will be offering and how you plan to prepare yourself for it. Because there are a million (at least) variables which could go into different business models, your best bet would be to start with an informal list. Here is an example of what I mean.

My business: Small engine repair

- Business location: Small shop rental in downtown area
- Rent for location: $300 monthly Utilities included except for phone. Length of lease / month to month
- LandLine Phone: $35 monthly
- Hours of operation
- Training manuals:
- Small engine repair
- Bookkeeping & accounting for the small business
- What type of business structure are you using
- Advertising for the small business
- Internet exposure for the small business
- How to outsource parts of your business
- How to find vendors for parts – both generic and brand name
- Pick up and drop off of customer's lawn mowers or other small engine items
- Cost sheet – each job will have its own cost sheet for labor and then parts costs and shipping. How are you going to provide a profit margin for buying new equipment or bonuses
- How long should each of these jobs take to complet
- Will I need other employees (Phone handling, mechanics, book-keeper, accountant)
- Will I be able to outsource or use contractors to do some of the jobs
- Payroll / Taxes - outsourcing to a payroll service or will I learn to do it yourself
- Keeping my schedule
- Tools inventory
- Capitalization funds for new tools, pre-pay parts and payroll
- Will I need a business loan

- What about licenses and insurance
- How much will I need to float for 6–8 months until I can build up a clientele

As you can see, your list may include all of these, and maybe many more. This is why we start outlining on paper. Your idea may be absolutely a fantastic one, but you don't want to be blindsided when finding out you need a "special license or permit" or a "special insurance". The excitement inside you will want to move forward just as quickly as possible and you can know you have done your due diligence to account for 95 to 100% of the steps needed to get your finances in order.

A very fatal move on the part of too many new business owners or entrepreneurs is "putting the cart before the horse". I mean that they are so excited about a great idea, new product or establishing a successful business, that motion begins before the plan has really been thought out. I hate to say it, but in many cases, knowledge of business necessities may come after the business ball has been rolling along for a while. Some of these can be very expensive and working capital may fall short because this issue was not investigated in the planning phase. This actually is the primary reason many businesses fail. There is under capitalization (not enough money) and incomplete planning.

Not many have the money to risk failure. Planning is the trampoline necessary to jump-start your idea. You simply just can't avoid it. Please don't try.

Do your due diligence in seeking information or personal one-on-one coaching when figuring your business plan. Let's not reinvent the wheel again, but allow those who have gone before share the essential information you need to avoid mistakes. I subscribe to a concept from my youth..... I had two older brothers. I watched them closely to see what got them in trouble and what didn't work. I chose not to follow in their footsteps. Instead, I made my own new mistakes. And you will too, but they will probably be less devastating. Trust me on this one.

Go find a template of a business plan on the internet. There are hundreds out there you can look at.

Making it Legal

Making it legal:

If your business plan is complete, you have the vendors lined up to provide your supplies and product and you have your funds to get started with reserves enough to handle unforeseen expenses, it is probably time to find out the licensing and insurance you need to avoid negative issues such as being closed down or sued. Forgive me, I am not trying to pop your euphoric entrepreneurship bubble here; just being very sensible in this day and age of lawsuits, etc. Find reputable insurance and bonding sources either locally or recommended by a business group you may be associated with.

Cities require businesses to be registered. This of course can cost anywhere from $50 to $$$ per year. Some charge according to how many you employ at your location; others may charge according to how many square feet your business occupies - you just have to check in with your city and find out. When speaking with them, it is always a great idea to ask, "what other types of licenses will I need for my new business which is opening soon"? One municipality always knows what other municipalities require for your business. Asking can be a nice time saver and often they are located close to one another.

You may also have licensing needed for County, State and of course Federal. Everyone gets a piece of you at one time or another. We all learn to play nicely in the business sandbox and be sure to play with everyone you should. Trying to avoid or ignore licensing will just come back to haunt you in the future. There could be fines and penalties due.

Just as a matter of irony, as I was securing all of the licensing for my office in the downtown section of my city, I asked what services did the city provide to me for having to buy a business license. The clerk looked at me and told me no one had ever asked that before. She was unable to tell me even after a 30 second empty look on her face. So I responded thusly, "I am paying for a business license to pay your salary, so you can issue me the business license"? She responded "I guess so".

The other item you do not want to forget or bypass is business insurance. If you have a business where your customers may be at your store location and someone falls and gets hurt, you will use your business insurance liability and bodily injury to cover them as needed. And, if they decide to sue you, this same insurance will pay to represent you and pay the award, if there is one. This policy also covers your business personal property. These items are your office supplies, tools, inventory, etc. If there is a fire, you will be glad you had this coverage. It can get you back up and running. Other business insurance may cover the work you have done or damages you could cause while doing the work.

I recall an insurance claim for $Millions when a repairman using a welding torch burned down three vegetable cold storage facilities which were bigger than football fields. I would have loved to be a fly on the wall when he got home and his spouse asked, "how was your day"?

Best be said that insurance is an extremely important item on your list.

Find someone who is very knowledgeable about business insurance and be sure to tell them EVERYTHING you intend to do in the scope of your business. Otherwise, you may find yourself high and dry with no coverage doing something you didn't share with the agent or insurance company.

Decision Making - Easy or Hard

Decision making - easy or hard:

When I think of a boss, I think of a person strolling around the place of business, looking over the comings and goings, seeing if the employees are doing their jobs and complimenting them, making small talk with the customers, smiling a lot and then going back into their office to play video games on their phone. Isn't that the idea which comes to your mind?

Alternatively there is the boss which is gruff and nasty - hair always needs combing, actions are jerky and voice is raised and threatening. This one runs around looking over everyone's shoulder and making negative comments about performance, threatening to fire someone and transforms immediately putting on a great big smile when a customer comes in. That boss virtually runs back to their office when the phone rings.

Whew! I prefer boss #1. It doesn't really matter whether this would be a man or a woman, there are great and poor bosses each. Only you can decide which kind of a boss you will be. I can tell you this, "you can catch a lot more flies with honey than with flypaper".

Each day you will experience ups and downs, you will see tremendous work from your employees and mistakes they will make. How are you going to respond? This is a step I don't see in written material. Being a boss is not being a little god, even if they think so. Be a boss which gets the respect and praise from employees and customers because you deserve it by treating folks with kindness and encouragement. If you think I am a push-over by suggesting that, you certainly don't know me. I am not a push-over. But I do know how to treat people so they have good self-esteem and will go full length to accomplish their employment tasks. You will want the same.

There are other decisions you will make along the way. These will impact to a small degree or to the critical degree of failure or success of your business. Scary. This is the life of an entrepreneur.

The more you are connected with your business, you may find decision making is a natural progression with time and experience. What I mean is this. When you are a parent, there are decisions you make for your kids daily - maybe multiple times daily. For the most part, you instinctively know what is good and what is bad. You may find running your business works like that too a lot of the time. But you must be connected - you have to have "skin" in it as well as your heart. Once you get to this point, you will know what I mean.

Systems

S**ystems:**

You may have never heard about "systems" but you work with them every day of your life. A system is simply a tried and true way to do something. It works so well that you repeat the process. Here is an example. You get up in the morning and make coffee. (Or maybe the night before). You never turn the pot on without putting in the water first - or you will burn up the coffee pot and ruin it. You must put in the coffee grounds or you will have hot water when you are done. A system is the process or order that you do things, like making coffee so it is basically the same every day.

Business works the same way. Say you are a retail store. One of your most important systems is monitoring the inventory so you do not run out of items which should be available for purchase. If a customer comes in looking for something and it is repeatedly not available, you will lose a customer to a store that has it.

When paying your bills, whether it be at home or at your business, you do it within a "system". There may be interruptions to the system such as not having enough money in your bank account to pay the bills. If that is the case, another "system" will come into play. Perhaps you will call the creditor and make other arrangements. Maybe you have a line of credit available for you to tap into to pay the bill and then pay the line of credit back at a later date. Perhaps you call Mom or Dad and hit them up for a loan. Whatever the solution is, you have a system to deal with the situation.

Systems in any business guarantee that information or products, employees or clients and customers are handled correctly. Systems set out the process and order in which to do things. That process is repeated time and time again because it has been tried and is true. When you have more than one person in the business, systems are of utmost importance. Everyone must know what they are supposed to do, and how to do it. Systems are constantly changing because the world around us changes. Saying "we always do it that way" just doesn't fly in today's business world.

I know this is a simplified overview of systems, but I think you get the idea. Companies put a lot of time and money into systems development to set the baseline for quality control in production as well as packaging and shipping. Employees receiving paychecks rely on the system of payroll to work. Any glitch in that system and everyone will hear about it!

Hiring Anyone?

Are you hiring staff, perhaps contractors, family members or going it alone?

Once you are at the point of launching your business, it will become obvious that you have to make another very large decision; are you hiring staff? If you hire folks and they are employees, there are additional expenses involved. There are employment taxes, workman's comp taxes (in case the employee gets hurt on the job), funding for insurances, retirement accounts and maybe even a membership to the health club! Yes, all of these items are tax deductible for your business, but what good is a tax deduction if you don't have the money to pay the employee?

Many years ago I had a medical transcription business which I ran out of my home and then an office location in the old downtown section of my city. My son was about 14 or 15 years old and was doing neighborhood lawn mowing to make money. We lived in a mild climate and the season for mowing lawns was longer than most and he enjoyed the $$ he got from his labors. He was rather faithful with that self-employment, so I opted to hire him taking completed medical transcription to the doctor's offices and bringing the new tapes for transcription back to me. I actually paid him a salary, although I didn't have to pay all of the taxes as he was my family member and there are certain exclusions for family members.

After a time he wasn't nearly as faithful to working for me as he was to his own lawn customers. He and I would have words about the need for consistency (systems again) and being there when the offices expected him and getting the new work back to me so I could start on it. I believe I hired and fired him at least 4 times. We were always good as parent and son, but I chose to no longer employ him - so I was back to doing it all myself.

There are pitfalls in hiring family members. There are definitely times when the family member takes liberties that a non-family person would not. There must be very clear lines as to what is expected and what will not be tolerated at the beginning of that employer/employee relationship. Remember that your business was YOUR idea. Family members take more liberty in telling you how to run your business. Be aware this is going to happen and have your response ready. You also must remember that your expectations cannot be unrealistic or of higher demand with a family member versus someone you hire whom you do not know.

There are other ways to get your jobs done also with less overhead and supervision. You can hire contractors if your business can perform without on-site employees. But please remember that a contractor has a definition according to the laws of the land. If you are calling someone a contractor to avoid taxes, but they are performing like an employee, be prepared to get caught. If it looks like a rose and smells like a rose, it must be a rose.

Here is the definition of a contractor: "The general rule is that an individual is an independent contractor if the payer has the right to control or direct only the result of the work and not what will be done and how it will be done. If you are an independent contractor, then you are self-employed." www.IRS.gov

To the contrary, according to the IRS: "You are not an independent contractor if you perform services that can be controlled by an employer (what will be done and how it will be done). This applies even if you are given freedom of action. What matters is that the employer has the legal right to control the details of how the services are performed."

Your company may benefit greatly with the utilization of contractors. Just be sure you know how to differentiate between an employee and a contractor. The IRS is always on the look-out for such things.

It is in your best interest to have a contract with the individual contractor defining "contractor" status, remuneration, etc. It is also a good idea to specify that as a contractor, you will not be paying for nor responsible for medical insurance, workman's compensation, etc. You can always consult an attorney for suggestions.

Bookkeeping and Accounting

Bookkeeping and Accounting:

An equally important system in your business is money handling. Money comes in and money goes out. That's the way of the world. But don't forget, when in business, a portion of that money is supposed to stop with you and stay in your bank account. That portion would be called "profit". If you don't make a profit, you will be an employee once again in the near future.

There are several ways you can perform the financial tasks so you have the information needed to determine your business financial health and when taxes need to be done and need to be paid. Taxation fuels this process. There are many different kinds of taxes and due dates associated with them. There is taxation you may pay when purchasing products or supplies. There is quarterly taxation on your profits - maybe gross profits. (I always had a problem with this as a gross profit is just the money you take in and is not offset by the expenses it costs to make the profit - but no one really cares about my feelings in this.) There are employee taxes which must be paid as scheduled. And then there are records to be kept of the payments and associated cause of the tax.

There are city, county, state and federal taxes. Believe me, everyone will get a little piece of your business. Keeping accurate and complete records of your income and your expenses is essential and critical in determining your profit margins and staying out of tax trouble. As I said earlier there are different ways you can do this. Software programs such as Quicken and TurboTax can take you through the entire process. Or, if you would like professional help, you can enlist the services of a bookkeeper and an accountant. Sometimes there is a mixture of both these.

Once again, entire books have been written about this topic. My goal here is to bring attention to the necessity of precision records keeping. Every expense and every income must be accounted for.

The information or reports generated by this process will aid in decision making for your business. It spells out how much you are profiting in your business and where you are not. Should you expand or should you hold. Can you buy a new piece of costly equipment, or should you lease it? The list goes on and on. Your financial report fuels the life of your business.

Keep your money intact in the business or you will find yourself without any emergency money which can lead to business death. I have seen entrepreneurs borrow money from the business or just plain take it out of the till so to speak. This is a very quick way to strip your business of its lifeblood. If a piece of equipment breaks down and needs repair or a "temp" must be hired to replace your employee who is home with Covid, all comes from the savings inside of the business. Having to resort to credit for such things increases the cost of the item and plays heavily on the small profit margin of a small business. Let your funds grow inside of the business and you will be prepared for most things which come along.

Conclusion

Conclusion:

I hope that you have found this guide helpful in getting an idea of the different facets of being self-employed or being an entrepreneur. There is definitely a romantic perception of "self-employment" which can rapidly vaporize once you realize what is at stake. There is money, time, future retirement, impact on family and friends, obligations to vendors and lessors. The list is long which causes a juggling act at times.

But don't forget why you are reading this and that you have a burning desire to be an entrepreneur. SUCCESS! Knowing that success is the result of your financial investment, organization, hard work, planning and sweat is amazing. Self-employment can be extremely fulfilling. And you may find, as I did, that "I am the best boss that I have ever had".

Welcome to my world!

About the Author

I am "few" years beyond a normal retirement age. In the course of my life I have had the pleasure of working in various capacities, all of which I totally enjoyed. I have been a bookkeeper, a para-educator, a receptionist (I did not blossom on this one), an insurance special accounts rep, an insurance agent, a trainer of medical computer applications for physicians and staff, a creator of medical templates, self-employed for 10.5 years providing medical transcription services and currently a retirement counselor who can help you develop your retirement plan beyond your finances; although I help there too.

I have always enjoyed being self-employed. I have told people for years that "I am the best boss I've ever had". My experiences over the years has been a gold mine. I will always be a student of new information and skills. My joy comes from sharing good things with people. Thank you for your purchase.